Armored

Elevator

Ryan Daley

BlazeVOX [books]

Buffalo, New York

Armored Elevator by Ryan Daley

Copyright © 2007

Published by BlazeVOX [books]

Printed in the United States of America
Book design by Geoffrey Gatza
Cover art by: Thomas Keeley

First Edition

ISBN: 1-934289-38-8   ISBN 13: 978-1-934289-38-9
Library of Congress Control Number: 2006940036

BlazeVOX [books]
14 Tremaine Ave
Kenmore, NY 14217

Editor@blazevox.org

publisher of weird little books

BlazeVOX [books]

blazevox.org

2   4   6   8   0   9   7   5   3   1

**a former incantation of, FLORIDA OCCUPIES ITSELF HATING THE HOMELESS, OR WAY TO GO UNDETECTED, was previously published in the Spring 2006 Edition of Blazevox online.

Table of Contents

s p u n k

Street Sweeper

Armored
Elevator

spunk

-for Michael Gizzi and Alex

Heya Mister, you've something on your wall.

-Graffiti in Quito, Ecuador

homecoming to a gangbang

Someone's *alma*
mater
white out its lettermen.
Picking one's
snout with sublime
finger puppets

Nothing needy
churchbound flu. One up
your melee. Broader
cross in sought
for highs and lows.

In weathered graffiti audible
dump trucks arrive
at newspaper's poor
day.

Erstwhile Uffizi seat
text wrapped fresco, monolithic
dressing as
your *pater*, pre-preening.

Knowing it will be misspelled, I get out of exit taxes.
Snuck by door. Father issues hard
wired into the wrist, a blanket spring.
What's with letting literary
figures kick.
It should be a fable bred forever.

I ask that you sacrifice me to the god of death

none jimmy a better mousetrap
with you slurping toilet water

        in a de-flanged hospital
reunited on a table
berserker eatery

fess to wit of
tongued it
adjust the frequency of Black Russians

contents of dumpsters
        rule in
        quiet leotards

their junk a flitter, who uses drugs in pink?

Poison Nightly

Jeremiad, answer your coercive
nitrates. It's golden.
Gotten away
from us.

Bots attacking old linksys
            goons creep past and up the columns
            greed in the expired marble, froze Gooden.

Wrap and guard for parlayed jaunts
into the new conjugal jingo
sucks to tailgate

step away from the vehicle

car alarms are
for the crows
crawl out of them

by the garbage, shadows
take a number

back into the smoked
mouth and out
annoyed slumber

¡chupame la malinche hijue-!

episiotomized doo-ragged and done that. Lamaze suavity
done levity, one more ant in the army to migrant

sometimes we draw sticks, others
weapons, gone and bruised our baddish

bodily
oolongs

five finger counts levy a legal fist
up doses they go in with wires
exit with a seat

don't lend simonizing to the Spaniards, their gist

a bonanza grouped in the democracy boulevard crew

they'll only enslave it and claim god on the record

"Independence is ours, puta" release the Diaspora
from the citation

run Macintosh
a swollen rhomboid takes on your phalanx
we could see dew on the dealership
busy with spray cans
Sweatier employers
Marsupial flavors
Spice racks

santa

It takes a village
           to sneer at
             you like that

Florida occupies itself hating the homeless, or way to go undetected

To mean bad weather I talk
like I have somewhere to be.

Rub hands [together
in a way
means you're busy]

It's so easy to get the building wrong
this is what my ex is supposed to look like
in the wheelchair
          doughy companion pushing

Why can their parlay not get moved
air out the matter there's
no ice cream to cry into

Assume the gumshoe position of
pissed rabbits in failed
pregnancy

Throw it in the bed
of the truck and
the gale will
blow it out.

candy striper

Not happy with spare tire

With everyone posed
holding a different
hose it's a wonder
we keep accessory
or assembly

Oh so
deluxe to
be raucous I am
a sexual predator

Because I am at your
feet this is
capitalization re-mulled

How the jelly warms.

untitled

1.

pall bears over minesweeper
country yourself behind

If only until its slogans born childish asterisks
shan't be ephemeral

they've gotten you in boxing
reared to compact mileage

there is integral emotion behind U-boats

hang the mixed panties on the grapevine,

oligarchs of zeppelin fans
the guzzlers enjoyed rebirth

2.

I spank your deity, who inhabits the cardboard outskirts
intrepid flavor crystals

pyramidal wrappers

printed corrections, we should kick
for theories of extra meat

sepia tone Italian Parliament jpegs but
cameras built for porn in Brazil

3.

research posed in robotic
suits the next crossover hit

sawdust of monoliths
to crosstrain
the appliances hum swords to Marxism
but only the swan hangs

mono charades into
totems the last known Toltec
lounge the head smoker coughs

in writing the view from a bike I
want out from under the bigtop's bogus poses
glow in no safer a paper route

your hooker looks
far from politics Pelé
pitches to remain my brother

why I'm not wearing
makeup at this hour

Uzbek the trilobite marathon, get
to Riker's the rub

outré lewd

My sphincter now aligns itself into attack formation.

Wonton-ly in-law

Love my perfect put-to-sleeper.

why you do not recycle packages of cigarettes

After two very uninspiring eggs
I'm now in print

Sass honest emptor
mister going to meet with my predatory editor
three piece aplomb
vexed by a slew of Lennon quotes

I took off your tunic and all I got was this slinky chemise

because there's a metal luge
when the white man got into jass

first to draw supine ran America
drill bits of which known by
gentry we've got egads

sky bind

any Doppler screen shot is fluke parallel
double magpies a toothless faux

two up top, one in the mete
            wee, prop up on
elmgrove to span floor to ceiling
fit together a way scrolled zines align

tardy for some tux, we come out of your
frigate with a more emperor jumpsuit

prix culture elbows after its cocker and cooption through
artifacts.

neat to see your trike
            at a site based in Chile
verted to metric
it's lonely to the catcher in high definition
            events dissolve into playbills

spiky telecom
skyscrapers
throwback to the 70s
feel locked in
lego gray, blocked pills

I'm rearranging my furniture inside you

which fit bests your syntax

russian gangsters on cruise ships
reaching international table turning
microphone smokes along to Helsinki our time:

dirigible gringos
resist gerbil Tupperware

shine in the creature light, dewy karaoke
one in line at the bar swoons

at this moment, the stuck watches
I'm fed to crocodiles
impressed by a number of toll tokens

cocked to sure up the info chunnel
I'm the fiber optic damsel
hidden in my tower with
disabled hard drives

jukebox stuck on the nearest Puccini algorithm
walking around in a Basque pith helmet
was kinda funny

this is for the people who perished in attempts toward a
hypermedia revival
crooners pile in

diddle infrastructure

Poetry gave her her
own particular
and she smeared it in
fries and not tested on animals under the exit sign

All pain is real usually
with airbrushed nipples

Why is this change of tenor allowed?

it's painted weather.
silence chow
jacked in hindsight
bellow
given,
tumbles off your palette like spouting *Lacan* in thick crayons

poetry of how much older in pounds
binge against a token
louder than the average hats off
to the perps decent
enough to dress us

semaphore

Trapped
          by triste nuance sound

of hurt things walked or was

    your web used car salesmen?

Between *lignes*,
          cessna humdinger
you end up lodged in the ass end.   Stress on
past

tense here, in bum fuck Egypt

        stretched to fit props
        so won't no offense.

           Nail pleases

tentacles in love.
          Rumple fuselage, get the hint I

avoid you

on right on the money, homeslice.

We got your problematic
                urchin.

Uncomfortably snuck underneath?

        Tartar entangled in
upright positraction

quibbles with raw format
enough around twice
because pass.
        I'm in church bell diapers. Respectfully tourniquet.

nightly through the Detectors

Trying to harbor
the perfect being
to make it
with high grade explosives

Voilà

I thought drugs that was the end.
History is you gaining weight.

don't look too *federal*

1.

Most dirty lyric is what gets kids
Illness spreads through
the keypad
but a status,
Hidden in snowsuits
Innuendo to be war

Prom a casa a tactile masterpiece
Glib to novel effects
National banks
Hardest thing to find a new
Doctor nowadays
dress down

2.

fade into remaindered Sasquatch

costume to prod
say no evidence.

admission, no
slip ups about

going cut
            time
out mother
my roomy
fleck

cause: no wonder why
people

hate jazz

ergonomic pax age of
the buck back
and forth

fistfight in
culture an already
say no

destroying the art of the western fuck

closer, Tlaxcaltec rummy

what makes those boats fatten their purpose

God ails whether and Lasorda

hydrate or launder.

favela your approximate q-tip

sonics jet the ledge and flunk

deed, hoist the flag from porch to gutter
it's too busy
giving away names
furnish network
calls for long coasts

oh no, for more illicit use

by the time the second tab makes
the esophagus I've got vitamins
from the cabinet of this
war hospital

make the portal fiat
salud Buenos Aires, parque
Lezama cross street
the angel of death
not hearing my ticker
thumbed thru lick

the page
Abaddon knelt, finger
holds the library up like
a basketball set you before

meanie

Lunchwave. Cellists into, sail.
Matter of generations. Greens
all the way. Binge . Ennui,
dolt. She makes it with
women at parties bite their
ears. Because text electronic
shower. Earth a wormy bot.
Violins that only in over
the falls.
Phenomenological
duct. Your mark
get set went. The garbage
men harbor calm at a time
in their loins. If you learn
one word at a time you shall never
be home, purloined kitty.
Language drops to your hands like
kids work. Toothy domino in Mid
English chair. Set against
wishes. Thunk out
like fog. Purge. I love I said.
Three card Monty. Back in deer.
Done horizontal chimney sweep. Being in points
south stretches
Bogart the effigy. My finger
shots the mother meat hooks she's
looking at you, killer. Expensive son
of instant magazine cover.
Refurb. Jism in digital Braille.
Presidential ikon is another spot on
the sheet. Just as I think the prom
dress is too quick. Sputter a hemmed over
end. Chance involvement
of mass. You bitten, then
bought. No queen.
Neuter. Screed of a yellow and

maritime tine. You touch it more
you want. I just hang on
way to marathon runs, not medium.
She pulls hair when the doll.
Object outline grown under the
fly. Coterie of alphabetical choir guys.
To scram in lower case. Cuddle
to scrutiny. Lint what's erased.
Tighten till hour to vacate audience. Nice
calves. Piece buddy. Better they
photocopy you and
yourn. Scrum trouble
for starters. Townsfolk and
city dwelt. Finger pointer.
Arbitrarily exempt sanctuary. Spaced
On power lines. Hasty cave napped
Meeting makes ends. The dominant
take on irreversible hootenanny. No
solace in the drunk bearing car.

bludgeon marathon

1.

With the advent of cellular trek
Humans as communicable

Sured up
ergo, snowballing might
adjunct to my sense of
self fellated

Swaps saliva linking the transcontinental

cable laid before the party you regret

2.

Blown in trousers
over the widget landscape
catcher palaver

Daisy cutters into your preschool tots
class room is when it rakes in theaters

Kodax of the clan, Byproduct

a picture tells 1000 words, few of which are
acid washed bobbies

when
      everyone picked
      on the bassoon

for being lightspeed tortoises

from zombies
amok to the drawing board
to commercial pilots
name the lisp
no, because
Strom Thurmond is no longer an adult
don't make it millennial

if words are what spacemen'll see in
spelunking we're goners

in poetry, Anselm, a recurring name.

not a weird question to beg
            door-to-door for burger

watch the hourglass not magnify the messiah

banging the hedges, time out in the dunes
tv spots empty of humor

outed furniture
worked in freelance
translation for NGOs in DC

"there is no sexuality in foreign airports"

the slang terminates the estuary,
rubbing hands
are the only kind to feather

a .357 to the head
ferrets its Goodyear

"there is no sense in Floridian carports"
so is the photo blurry cause you're crying?

rumble strips

Mixing the furnishings
to create
indents

"Tears stream down
the face. Mucus stopped
up runny
nose. A ring under
after we take it, cough
and gag,"

College kids rappel their own

untitled

Station when chain smoking
coalition of cassette ere metal detector
            even with your beef behind it, nothing
            given to the lectern

Being a barber at age fifteen
military elephants crossed the Guadalquivir with cornets
            novel to the text
Whose captors supplant on embouchure
chassis nature neon bares us
The bully wrapped in the x-axis wasn't
            torn in two from lunch hour chests
And a tree in trying

Want narrative write it in cable
            on the nation's mighty underlings

A who's who in New York without
lungs

Surfaces on the moon too serious for his trench coat

Called to task an afternoon we leaders
            Confront basics of writing in plastic
She calls in twenty cent wings

Interloping of
emergency call boxes as low impact theater

why are the pictures of the twentieth
century the same?
It's like rice
pudding, only
the French can

now save us.

snuff film

Pachyderm largesse
buxom fogging up
the lens
the foul seduces.

Fire
alone saves.

The land in ducats
because I'm tired of it

Street Sweeper

But at times
a helping of tenderness is not enough
and it's necessary to add
a helping of lead.

-*Santiago Feliú*

Going subcommando

Far souped up ride the mural, I've found Jesus.
When lit, bang pots and par on the course.
Subcomandante's rpg converts to raw
but the country club wood is sunk

Marcos in drag. Urge
antenna windward. What banana seated-
diktat.

A guess 'em way to go in your pants.
A' push it real good! Spot me, vato.

On Marcos' lap, cameras angled away.
His hungry alien torso (not shown) perplexed the press.

Antes del fin, the mass shit cous'
jacks the copse.
Boss icons are burned and pissed on.

An effigy generally burns with a long stinger and
invalid membership ID.

Spoke n' Sez:

I am too home painting my nails
with Bite Free to be
three hundred and twenty third
Instant Breakfasts of Chuck Norris

perhaps it's the Revlon,
bench pressing in boxers
don't bunch

piano falling versus man equals cosine
dragnets get you ill, dig?

can I touch you there, S-s-sire? There
where your crossbars
dawdle
where a furry pay for toil

pokes your head
in the toilet so often
checks for invaders

a pop collar
releases the hydrant I
am woman, and bass

Runt

we should stop recycling.
no we shouldn't, we must do
we should stop kissing
while chewing our food.

Terra Cotta Little Richard

What a high life he's got
Richard just won't take the Ryder
and clones himself smocks, Tarkovsky's
spooged plants,

clay over the causeway
let out of your sight he perishes.

--

pulling out the Ford Falcons, folks
pull the lever or no?

Chevy Chase on drums, Brinks on syths
three-sixty floats of emergency

don the audio

--

over the telecom
your curves make espaghetti
for six
        nuf?

boca de baño

adioses
high gloss shows
in Ringling

airbrush the shoe
I'm planting on
your face

oh, meaning frescoes

one eight
hundred eat
my dong

sedentary prow

chafes my pits
to speed full ahead in plastic chinstrap

eons beyond
a playground brawl

lying on your
back beaten the shit out of
in foreign area code you say let's trade sneaks

baltasar garzón

before the Spanish
courts get carried away--
take the pennants-- I'll say-- to
throw cellmates into lye

only preps the perps for
if you suck hard cherries fall off

[my father smears meat inside
coats says it keeps
cops from knocking]

Olé

-for Alex

conveyor into the cold sweat
your crack, my palpitations

a swoon no por favor please
choose Vivaldi and soda, mayor
no mistake, we're unequivocal:
that clock tower is Belgian.

Epoxy of cows, slink in that half
light gin, near clack belongs

plots for the codas rabble provosts
smack dab boats
dot the urethra how like a turtle

I found you there
C is for cookie, in un-twatonic statehood.
my margins brought, catch this deafening thighs

skybox

-for Kent

Nothing a greater shove than the Força de F
unstoppable in their leisure suits
velvet rope take us seriously, porfa!
like giant aspirin on a liver sprain
within the diamond rations of the FDA

We quipped about bags
that it's for Chex
fuses a holiday odor
which don't mamma early on
until knighted by forest crits
as kindred bag folk
finger lone hooks,
"line up"

Icy as Spanish pudding, my vulva
must solve by matching escapes
--a genius done in tempo with death metal—

Craving a spreadsheet of metro north
sandwiches for rodents, não, wedgies
ptarmigans ace bees please
repeat the word use it
gun my lats in
successfully, but
salve, salve, a flop pension

63

Nome

Somewhere - rains
shove
from Chi-town waits for it.
Glazed.
Dos, porfis.
Humming under the el. No, not
Lawrence Tribe
again. A judge, née segundo.
Dejé el fucking wallet. Supped
into dusk,
later than gone neon.

clown joke #2

-for Kaps

fuck you clown and
bigtop you spray painted the bus on,
no room? on to Bethlehem
find a Sharpie
poodles vote you ugly
the longest dark talkie

clown fuck Parker Posey.
Clean but oh no spread not the sofa.
Her poodle underwear
of the soft millennium. Bad Doors
transformers, more than meets
your internet, steals your preggo
fax nails tossed into wastebaskets
that fade
a mark: markie
but you'll sniff it, fuck
you clown

history of dozers

1.
the "small of the back" is worn out

outpouring
ingredients into that cake
and still no guests

waiter, a civilization armed to the tent
in my kicker, why not puto?
because it's from Kroger?

brats can hang themselves in cords

unaware of kilter
grass a harpie
to solder more ocean

lockers of Orleans, aflame! traffic
pops in your face

grab some ass and a foldie chair

2.
saunter via deserts some manna, stat

rinse the iodine off like parking a Taurus
cradle cap suits the ban
your halls prohibited the T-shirt

we snip with antique sleight
Grummond to the river
he dwelt in launder

after the milk ruins
does the claymation push through the onlookers
snorkle out what's albacore

mete brims with razed characters
so how's the mural drown

coffee?
masons?

whip yours out.

3.
pejorative to say cottage
in a drama gait
cajoler embouchure
sans whammo
dogs sail long

pauses in the globe caught
you quenched with fountain lips
and under the sundresses
sluts kiss the hertz

4.
summer clean,
doornail cats
         off the chain without a Hollywood Darjeeling

drag your ass to the aisle's end for frozen stuff
if you aren't against the fad
tag, it's in your grill.

the flight of Elton John into Apollo

What phallic moonstruck mon
cher could fix this car stereo
and board the ocean liner to
amped for sailors bars rain
and the prostate beacon of
Bacon, soixante-
neuf bright, bushy

a downtown bistro has it,
the new vinyl copy of opt
sons,
shucks I'm holding
the door, man the ultra
slim razors!

Rant

between good head
they manhandle Sloth
once testosterone says moo
with spray disinfectants
we never again double
back on your senses.

indeed, the popping
stops of automated moles
wins trinkets that
glossaries slobber, "bifurcate."

My 15-year-olds in Handan hadn't much trouble

slipping it out
no crops, expect fruit pectin

gaper, a rubber prefect union,
judge though revolving
spigots gets deportivo

ruminate the scape o'er
if your girl steps up
second hand parks
lots of cafe
scorch, borscht
brag Dutch vice

the photographed
sort barbells

judging by submarines
pact: learn
some gordito cheats
on the escalator

Pavers

Botox can be found in nature, squirrels
have found a way to play nice

amphibious SPF to gated
landing craft for the pros of soil
reinforce the acorn

"home you
go pilgrim" hotels to your
algal bloom a moot snubs

"keep those critters outta my sight" we're
working Rome here so

my neighbor
the schmuck parks
blocking my apron but
thanks be my turtles are AIDS-free

DeBeers

the mere mention of
forever fills a museum of natural history
the subway runs from thyroid to metatarsel
(upgrade with equipped hit points)
if snipped, this could mean no marriage, no booty
autumn a brilliant time for (taking advantage of) return slips

spending forever in the mouth of a slave, happy,
singing sang out over the delta, privileged
to wear such glee on your finger. Watch it
glitter bro

Flummox Weatherly

-for Thom Keeley

"By covering with fat and wrapping him" in
grocery, a player gains points
plastic bags usually crouch the entrance to the
laser

sworn into a juke, the Messerschmitt evaded
countless parties.

Jump Ms. Croft, into your nightie.

Ich bin ein monstrous. Loose-toed nanny.
Follow, my heart strands. Its strange stagecoach
alighting into caught death of cold.

A bogus mail collection tiara worn above the pits'
smock appears.

Ants emerge from a seal fissure in quicksand.

Gent

go lightly, worms torn corners
up and with scimitars,
walk out glaring
peace keepers
plunge into the jungle gym
fungal at the sit-in
pop sensibility
training of the cock

welcome to the Jehovah's Witnesses touchscreen
-for Mike Magee

contents under spraypainted
graffiti into sod
hung on the wall,

how about
concrete? how about
moveable players?

clumsy with the joystick
noggin it's your boy toy
into fudged runtime environs

tonight I write the saddest ad
copy, far off a boy throws jai alai
pelotas into a gang

fiesta on the barge
tonight at six
black trousers, white shirt
I snooze at the wheel
oh my tyrant, weld
eggshell sheen
sold to finicky

how much
longer will I be able
to inherit a Krispy Kreme franchise?

irony states guts are Italian

favor in lipstick factories
for their presidency and hue
of media grappa
torn on who to Pert
and in what Motel 6
covered dumpsters

plus phone operators
the sack shape entirety of fetus
cargo no more
glyphs bellyache because
with a nose jamb
Robespierre skulks, says
He'd rather open a branch
than subtract aristocrats

Guest

in the blush moonlight
I hit and hit and hit
and hit you I hit
and hit and hit
and hit
you
are my favorite drum

collapsible hardware coffins

this couplet heaved up
and placed into the bed of your
F-150, which,
hauled over hairpins,
called for a slew of operating systems
running diagonal audits
sures up the clutches of
acreage and aging formula
mellow in mid-concourse, bags
useless in the arms, expires
a gasp radar pinpoints out in a sea
of aflame defective Firestones.

Gun control

bigger than a molecular Texas
Ryan and the sphinx make friends

the chapel is killing me, its wank apex
the sad fact there's stilts
discolored, faux like a boner

a sorry Gacy
hidden in the bushes, he tears underwear torn
born again little shit
who likes short shorts I bought in King of Prussia

Shanghai your reuben,
ease your mpegs round petrol

some fuck dressed in wu-tards, pirouettes-
don't ever thumb the wad on the nightstand

Sprawl

using the roundabout
for featured purposes
we spot vagrants
to avoid collage

base the loofah on fused manifolds
sprawling colony sacks the lapsed catholic
die-cast you lout, she's my
carnival ride or
suits astronauts wear
in vague -pop hands off-
idiom should
if the Lazyboy

They assume it's politics it's not.

if you see the urinal mat next to me He has appeared
His people culminating in visits to earth in the flesh when
He was killed for our nonpareils and his snickers.
Zapatos? Made for cents.

Fucktard, sneer kids. Deceased persons die in a
crash, dormant in accounts.
Allow Democrats to run
pro-family platforms hey those aren't faithful
Your offspring gave up their rubbers to support you.
Would an apparation in the sky help? Fingerfood?

During our investigation and auditing in a bank,
naturally the emperor knew the instructions
my dept. fast forwards to Luke. As always
his points are humorous, but don't miss a valid money shot
out a cow into FUNDS WITH THIS BANK WITHOUT
crabs in family court booze before our discovery
that pants lead to development.

the serial print down the shaft is invented later
and recorded in the Qur'an, concerning GWAR.
In the beginning was the logos, and the logos is a Sebring.

complex narration thru lots

I remain,

    Wading through melons
[tranquilo, they will not cease to study English]
breathe less in

                traffic

the tide

de-luge entire villages
native themes of numerous medaled postdocs

Question facial growth and biopic directors

infinite apes tap out the Chaucer, yawning
ergo I Dunlop

hillocks
Magneto alarm clocks

swing your superhero into
locked positive
rowboat of the atom

hitching digits in Francaise
robotics value lifeblood, rudder fractions

in the white room: cakes, towel racks, comped dixie cups

remorse, I only possess one action figure
to gripe from one's country

It's bollucks. Waste manages.

The Jetsons don't flush.
Virginia with earnest answers
as to why you're both preggers

**release the diaspora from the kiddy pool citation,
detail: frat**

canton, breakfast pinch your bubbas
the less your sonar floats lady
of sweet blue Jesucristo
a main bloke
hoaxer San Diego Charger
part of expat
sidewalk rascals deploy
the centerfolds teaming
with gel inserts

feet locked in
imposter slalom

souced, mince vexed
the troop ships
throat but mag wheels swallow
and take up the sea
watchwords, manhunts
lone columbine
after a day, fish
can witness pre-fizz
to parry the rooster of fameless bytes

Es un miamor

fought to rid myself of
her her
name a dimple
that knows each cat and
service stamps in
nylon and how it's used

oh please no Miro

some like candy,
others
el niño.

one is not required to eat Lucky Charms

it's cute you hear

-for Charles Stotler

to pick the Yale, cover your pin

I've expelled the large wrestler into the basin
my glock, plea—
I'll wallop every geezer in this piece

but if doesn't last through a haircut,
harbor mass garçon

the passage of time is figured by piano
snowballing in atrophy, nave of rockets

just by looking at Casablanca I know they're carrying
eddying a version

She quips if I spayed mayday a nude couplet
out the slow gate to garnish UV

the spectrum of limos a tenor lingus

Hazmat

eck. cradle warm eggs under
your tongue
dress fetid for candy
land give it a dram

asked to annoint the city in green river goo
Paddy, mime the next verse,
foul the loo, twinkies are for birds

parking your metal decoder in reserve plays
spotted odor, flame fiancées at twice the sun's lit

what winks back from your fuckhole matter
a quick adder the rubber before the tanks crusher

our prime minister stains this mortal fish pant
credit slits in quack
lack ick, a sack of turds lip-smacked
…delish!

Ryan Daley likes East Providence. But not as much as he likes to partake in the bi-monthly fundraiser, *Coloring for Anarchy*. He is an M.F.A. candidate at Brown University.

End Credits

I would like to think that the following individuals played no small part in aiding and abetting: Robert and Shelley Daley; siblings Caitlin, Eileen Liz, Patrick (especially for his adroit use of trial versions of Photoshop); Alex Sears, Michael Gizzi, Mike Magee, Kent Johnson, Thom Keeley, Charles Stotler, David Kaps, Tatiana Morales Azofeifa, Brianna Colburn, Michael Coppola, Nicole Dutton, Daniel Howe, Mike Kim, Michael Stewart, The Acuña Muñoz Family, Alfredo Vindas Castro, Caroline Whitbeck (for the "jelly" edit), Luis Chavez Miranda, Wen Hsu Chen, Vanessa Hsu Chen, Brian Kim Stefans, Rebeca Hernandez, Forrest Gander, Keith Waldrop, Kate Schapira, Bronwen Tate, Tod Edgerton, Lynn Xu.

Many thanks for your patience and skillful bribery of the appropriate government entities.

Made in the USA